Time to try....

the Alkaline Diet

Nourish, Heal & Restore Balance To Your Body

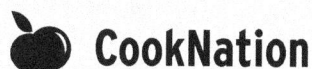

CookNation

Time to try... the Alkaline Diet

NOURISH, HEAL & RESTORE BALANCE TO YOUR BODY

ISBN 978-1-912511-80-8

DISCLAIMER

CONTENTS

Dinner Recipes

Soup Recipes

Dessert Recipes

Snack Recipes

Homemade Extras

INTRODUCTION

The Alkaline Diet is a proven approach to looking after your body, and mind, keeping disease at bay whilst boosting energy levels and optimising the digestive and immune systems.

The significance of health, nutrition and lifestyle have become increasingly focussed over recent years with their importance resonating more strongly now than ever before. A new generation is inspiring the masses, shining light on decades of research and imposing a consciousness of just how important what we eat is for our bodies and long-term health. As much as diets have been utilised to reduce fat, weight and boost immune systems over time, 'diet' is now being rightly recognised as a lifestyle; understanding nutrients and how foods affect our bodies and wellbeing. In a world full of confectionery and processed food, diets are now beginning to change, reversing back to basics with the health benefits plentiful. The Alkaline Diet offers just that; a proven approach to looking after your body, and mind, keeping disease at bay whilst boosting energy levels and optimising the digestive and immune systems. The Alkaline Diet is simple, but effective and easy to implement into your day-to-day lifestyle.

The key to improving your overall health and losing excess weight is to understand the digestive system: how it works; how your body digests food; and how your body copes with and responds to certain foods. When your digestive system is working properly, countless health issues can be aided, minimised, prevented and sometimes completely eradicated. Optimising your digestive system is the first step to better health and the Alkaline Diet helps you to do just that.

The Alkaline Diet is essentially underpinned by one of the most basic and simplistic sciences - pH levels. pH levels are effectively a spectrum or a scale, with acidic at one end, and alkaline at the other. We know that certain foods are harder for our bodies to digest and process, which can lead to a sluggish system and unnecessarily stored fats and acids, among a number of other health issues, such as bloating and indigestion, for example. Other foods are more efficiently processed by our bodies, resulting in a cleaner, healthier digestive system.

ACIDIC
VS.
Alkaline
FOOD

PH SPECTRUM

The pH scale is between 1 to 14 units. Above 7 is considered alkaline and below acidic. Most vegetables are 7 and above while meat, processed sugars and alcohol are all below 7 (see chart on previous page).

As with all things, diet, lifestyle and wellbeing are all about balance. Whilst alkaline foods are generally best for our bodies, elements of more acidic foods are still often required for the body to properly function. Scientists and researchers commonly propose that two thirds of your plate should be filled with alkaline foods, with the remaining third allowing for foods slightly more acidic.

Understanding food and their ranging alkalinity or acidity is essential as many foods or drinks that fall into a typical day-to-day diet, even for the more health conscious of us, are actually highly acidic. Obvious to some, alcohol, fast food and fizzy drinks are all highly acidic, however, less obvious acidic foods are your morning cup of coffee, tea or orange juice, your brunch pastry, your shop-bought sandwich for lunch, and even the biscuit you snack on without thought when returning home. Unnecessary intakes of highly acidic foods can easily creep into your diet and make hard work for your digestive system. The Alkaline Diet focuses on balancing this back out. Therefore, it is important to recognise that it is not just food that can be acidic to your body creating negative effects. Equally, lack of exercise and stress can have a huge impact on the body, and even with the healthiest of diets can still weigh us down, quite literally both physically and mentally.

It is important to include exercise in your daily life: this does not need to be high intensity gym classes, or training for a marathon. Walking or cycling rather than driving, taking the stairs rather than the lift or a brisk walk, can all get your blood moving around your body, energising you enough to positively impact your lifestyle. Small changes are often the most significant.

Additionally, whilst small amounts of stress are thought to be good for us by scientists, motivating us to achieve, too much stress is arguably an unhealthy and harmful thing for our bodies, as well as our minds. Finding tools to appropriately manage stress and enable you to relax, unwind and switch off is quite simply invaluable; releasing these negative feelings and toxins can immediately improve your overall health, not just your digestive system.

An Alkaline Diet can not only dramatically benefit your digestive system, but is also understood to keep you looking younger for longer, improve your quality of sleep and boost your energy levels. Improving alkalinity levels in your diet has a significant impact on your skin, as well as your nails and hair, providing them with a rejuvenated appearance aiding growth, hydration, strength and overall appearance. Clearer, healthier skin and radiant looking hair are often one of the first changes noticed when switching to the Alkaline Diet with the benefits taking effect surprisingly quickly.

Naturally, reducing your intake of acidic foods such as caffeine and sugar fuelled drinks helps to maintain your blood sugar levels and regulate your energy levels throughout the day. It is quite incredible the impact that this simple change can have on your health and wellbeing when your body is not subjected to a rollercoaster of caffeine and sugar rushes, highs and consequent crashes and lows. Such effects of the Alkaline Diet roll over into many other aspects of your health and life through this improved consistency.

All of these benefits can consequently help you to lose excess weight and maintain your healthy, goal weight. The balance and moderation of the Alkaline Diet makes this much more achievable and very minor, simple changes in your lifestyle and cooking can help improve your health in the long-term.

One of the key things to remember with the Alkaline Diet is quality over quantity: good quality meats and products are much better for your system than their cheaper, value alternatives. If eating meat, fish and animal products, choose organic and free-range products of the best cut and quality. This should ensure limited, if any, use of pesticides and chemicals leaving the product purer, Often meat products such as minced beef and sausages include additional fats and highly acidic extras, for example. The same concept applies to all foods, even vegetables, fruit and herbs - the fresher the better.

An alkaline diet mainly takes you back to basics with cooking; cooking from scratch and with the best, freshest and least tampered with products, rather than completely eliminating certain foods or food groups like other short-term diets may suggest. Food should be balanced and in moderation. The typical modern, western diet sees the population eating far more meat and protein than necessary, so whilst it is not essential to remove such foods and products entirely from our diets, the concept of quality over quantity is ever more important.

pH levels are formed across a scale, so foods are not automatically one or the other, as this can depend on how the food has been grown, treated, fed and/or ripened, however, some typical examples of alkaline and acidic foods are as follows.

- **Highly acidic foods** are processed foods,
- Fast food and refined sugars, including alcohol, coffee, and refined flour, such as with breads, cakes and typical sweet treats.
- Additionally, animal protein is also generally highly acidic, whether beef, lamb, chicken or pork, or even fish, as well as matured and aged dairy products and cheeses.
- Fresh dairy products and cheeses are a better option as they are mildly acidic, although unpasteurised dairy products are the best option, if suitable and available.

- **Highly alkaline foods** are, as most likely expected, almost all vegetables and most fruits.
- Herbs and most spices are highly encouraged as well; these can add great flavour to recipes and are an excellent way of enhancing a meal and flavour without distressing your body with typically acidic foods that may have otherwise been used.
- As is the nature of the spectrum, some are of course better than others,
- Root vegetables such as carrots & potatoes and spices, seeds & nuts such as fennel, ginger and quinoa are some of the most alkaline foods.
- Other specific examples of wonderfully alkaline foods are kale, pumpkins, coconut, broccoli, mango, avocado and beetroot.

Another crucial element of the Alkaline Diet is to enjoy your food. Even the most alkaline shopping lists, stocked cupboards and freshly prepared diets can have their good sourcing and preparation undone by rapidly eating your meals, taking little time to thoroughly chew, enjoy and digest. Food that is not chewed properly will make even the most efficient digestive systems struggle, undoing your hard work. Remember, the Alkaline Diet is more than just a diet - stepping back, slowing down and taking your time can sometimes be the best thing for you. In today's frantic world this may be difficult to do but is one of the most effective things you can do for your health and wellbeing.

Our re-balancing recipes are delicious, easy to follow and the perfect way to balance alkaline and acidic foods. Eating predominately vegetarian foods will make it easier to maintain an alkaline balance however if you like meat and fish try to follow an 80/20 rule with the majority of your plate filled with vegetables and whole grains and the balance with protein rich meat or fish.

Breakfast
RECIPES

Time to try....

SUMMER FRUIT PORRIDGE

Ingredients

- 100g/3½ oz gluten free porridge oats
- 175ml/6floz hemp milk
- 25g/1oz dried mango
- 25g/1oz dried apricots
- Pinch of chia seeds

Method

1 Mix the porridge oats and milk in a saucepan on a low heat.

2 Stir until the mixture begins to thicken and the oats soften.

3 Either add in the dried fruit and continue to stir until warmed through or add the dried fruit on top when serving.

4 Sprinkle on the Chia Seeds to serve.

CHEF'S NOTE

Oat milk, Nut milk or Soya milk can be used as alternatives for the Hemp milk; similarly, replace the dried Mango and Apricots with your choice of dried, or seasonal fresh, organic fruit for a variety of fruit porridge breakfast options.

MIXED BEANS ON TOAST

Ingredients

- 2 tsp almond butter
- 50g/2oz tinned red kidney beans
- 50g/2oz tinned lima (white) beans
- 50g/2oz tinned black-eyed peas
- 150g/5oz chopped tomatoes

- 1 tsp mild chilli powder
- ½ tsp paprika
- Salt and pepper to season
- 2 thick slices of gluten free, seeded bread
- Parsley to serve

Method

1 Heat 1 teaspoon of the almond butter in a saucepan on a low heat.

2 Add into the pan the beans and chopped tomatoes and allow the mixture to simmer for 5 minutes, gently stirring to ensure the mixture does not stick.

3 Stir in the chilli powder, paprika and salt and pepper and continue to simmer on a low heat for another 5 minutes, or until the beans are cooked.

4 Toast the gluten free bread and spread on the remaining almond butter.

5 Pour the bean mixture on top of the toast and add a garnish of parsley to serve.

CHEF'S NOTE
Beans act as a fantastically filling breakfast option for cold, winter mornings to fuel your body for a busy day ahead.

COCONUT PORRIDGE

Ingredients

- 100g/3½oz gluten free porridge oats
- 175ml/6fl oz almond milk
- 50g/2oz shredded coconut
- 1 tsp coconut flakes
- 1 tbsp almonds, crushed

Method

1 Mix the porridge oats and milk in a saucepan on a low heat.

2 Gently stir until the mixture begins to thicken and the oats soften.

3 Stir in the shredded coconut and warm through.

4 Sprinkle the coconut flakes and crushed almonds on top to serve.

CHEF'S NOTE

Nuts offer a wealth of nutrients and are a great alkaline addition to any meal to add and enhance flavour.

SUPER GREENS AND MUSHROOM BREAKFAST

Ingredients

- ½ tbsp flaxseed oil
- 8 asparagus spears
- Pinch of sea salt
- ½ tbsp hempseed oil
- 100g/3½oz button mushrooms, chopped
- ½ clove of garlic, crushed

- 150g/5oz fresh spinach
- 2 large handfuls of fresh rocket leaves
- ½ tbsp pine nuts
- 1 tsp flax seeds
- 1 tsp hemp seeds

Method

1 Pre-heat the oven to 180C/350F/Gas4.

2 Drizzle half the flaxseed oil on a baking tray.

3 Place the asparagus stalks on the tray and drizzle the rest of the oil over the stalks. Season with sea salt and place in the oven to roast for 15 minutes, or until tender.

4 Warm the hempseed oil in a saucepan over a medium heat.

5 Place the chopped mushrooms into the pan with the garlic and stir together. Allow the mushrooms to cook for a few minutes, or until soft, stirring them every now and again.

6 Add in the spinach and cook for further 2 minutes until the spinach has softened and wilted into the mixture.

7 Use the rocket leaves as a base to serve. Lay the grilled asparagus on the rocket bed, spooning the mushroom mixture on top.

8 Sprinkle over the pine nuts and seeds to serve.

CHEF'S NOTE

Hemp seeds are exceptionally nutritious and great to add into any seed mix to add texture and key nutrients to finish almost any meal.

SUPERCHARGED TOMATOES ON TOAST

Ingredients

- 2 beef tomatoes, finely chopped
- ½ tbsp flaxseed oil
- 1 Garlic clove, crushed
- 1 tbsp vegan red pesto
- Sea salt and pepper to season

- 2 slices of seeded, gluten free bread
- Pinch of pumpkin seeds
- Pinch of flax seeds
- Pinch of chia seeds

Method

1 Mix the tomatoes with the oil, garlic and pesto until a chunky mixture forms.

2 Season well with sea salt and pepper.

3 Grill or toast the bread, turning to ensure an even, crispy finish.

4 Spread the tomato mixture onto the toast and top with the mixed seeds to serve.

CHEF'S NOTE

Add some fresh chillies to the tomato mixture to accelerate your metabolism and tingle your taste buds.

MASHED BANANA AND BLUEBERRY YOGHURT

Ingredients

- 2 ripe bananas
- 2 tbsp coconut cream
- 75g/3oz blueberries

- 1 tbsp almonds, crushed
- 2 tbsp pecan nuts to serve

Method

1 Use a fork to mash the ripe bananas into a lumpy mixture.

2 Then, simply fold in the coconut cream and blueberries.

3 Sprinkle the crushed almonds and pecan nuts on top to serve.

CHEF'S NOTE

For a busy on-the-go alternative, add Coconut or Almond milk and blend into a smoothie to kick start your day.

SMASHED AVOCADO BRUSCHETTA

Ingredients

- 2 ripe avocado peeled, de-stoned and mashed
- 1 large ripe beef tomato, finely diced
- ¼ garlic clove, crushed
- 1 tsp freshly squeezed lime juice
- Pinch of sea salt

- 1 tbsp coriander, finely chopped
- 1 tsp avocado oil
- 2 thick slices of sprouted wheat bread
- ½ tsp dried chilli flakes
- 1 tsp chia seeds

Method

1 Place the mashed avocado, diced tomato and garlic into a bowl and combine together.

2 Add the lime juice, sea salt, coriander and oil into the avocado mixture.

3 Lightly toast the sprouted wheat bread and then gently spread the avocado mixture on top.

4 Sprinkle over the chilli flakes and chia seeds to serve.

CHEF'S NOTE

Avocado is considered an alkaline superfood, it is packed with antioxidants and can be easily incorporated in lots of breakfast recipes.

STRAWBERRY AND MANGO COMPOTE

Ingredients

- 150g/5oz ripe strawberries
- 100g/3½oz ripe mango, diced
- 1 tsp coconut palm sugar

- 120ml/4floz fresh, natural yoghurt
- 1 tbsp rye flakes
- 1 tbsp chia seeds

Method

1 Remove the green tops from the strawberries and roughly chop.

2 Mash the chopped strawberries and mango together and stir in the coconut palm sugar.

3 Spoon the mixture into a bowl or glass and top with the fresh, natural yoghurt.

4 Sprinkle over the Rye Flakes and Chia Seeds to serve.

CHEF'S NOTE

Eating ripe foods is important and so varying this with seasonal alternatives is a great way to ensure you are eating the right fruit at the right time of year when it is at its very best.

SUPER SEEDED ORANGE YOGHURT

Ingredients

- 1 tsp freshly squeezed orange juice
- 150ml/5floz fresh goat yoghurt
- 1 tbsp pumpkin seeds
- 1 tbsp sunflower seeds
- 1 tsp flaxseeds
- 1 tbsp pecan nuts, chopped or crushed
- 1 tsp chia seeds
- Orange zest to serve

Method

1 Stir the freshly squeezed orange juice into the goat's yoghurt and place to one side.

2 In a separate bowl, mix the seeds and pecan nuts together.

3 Spoon the yoghurt into a bowl or glass to serve and top with the seed mixture (or if you prefer; stir the seed mixture into the yoghurt and mix well before serving).

4 Sprinkle a small shaving of orange zest on top to serve.

CHEF'S NOTE

This is a fantastic seed mix that can be used to supercharge spreads and porridge. If you prefer to grind the seed and nut mixture, this can easily be done with a coffee grinder or pestle and mortar.

SUPER SIMPLE AVOCADO EGGS

Ingredients

- 1 large ripe avocado, halved and de-stoned
- 2 large egg yolks
- 1 tsp flaxseed oil
- Sea salt and pepper to season
- 1 tsp flaxseeds
- Freshly chopped flat leaf parsley to serve

Method

1 Pre-heat the oven to 180C./350F/Gas4.

2 Place each avocado half on a baking tray and add an egg yolk into the small hole where the avocado seed would have been embedded.

3 Drizzle the flaxseed oil over the avocados & eggs and season with sea salt and pepper.

4 Place in the oven and cook for 15 minutes.

5 Remove from the oven and top with the flaxseeds and freshly chopped parsley to serve.

CHEF'S NOTE

Feel free to double up the quantities if you want an even more substantial start to you day.

TRADITIONAL ENGLISH EGG MAYONNAISE SARNIE

Ingredients

- 4 slices of seeded, gluten free bread
- 1 tbsp homemade mayonnaise (p93)
- A small handful of watercress
- 3 large eggs, hardboiled & shelled
- Sea salt and pepper to season

Method

1 Lightly spread the slices of bread with homemade mayonnaise.

2 On two of the four slices sprinkle on the watercress to evenly cover.

3 Chop the hardboiled eggs and place on top of the watercress.

4 Season with salt and pepper and add the remaining two slices of bread on top to complete the sandwich.

CHEF'S NOTE
Serve with a small portion of homemade root vegetable crisps (p82).

Lunch
RECIPES

Time to try....

MUSHROOM AND HUMMUS PITTA

Ingredients

- 2 gluten free pitta breads
- 2 tbsp homemade hummus (p90)
- 2 handfuls of fresh watercress
- 2 large mushrooms, finely chopped
- ½ fresh, ripe avocado, peeled, de-stoned and cubed
- Pepper to season

Method

1 Lightly toast or grill the pittas, just enough for them to begin to gently separate.

2 Spread the hummus on the insides of the pittas.

3 Fill with the chopped mushrooms and avocado.

4 Season with pepper and serve.

CHEF'S NOTE

Use whichever type of mushrooms you prefer. Portobello are a good choice.

CHICKEN AVOCADO AND CARROT WRAP

Ingredients

- 2 sprouted wheat wraps
- 1 tbsp dairy-free mayonnaise
- 2 handfuls of watercress
- 1 chicken Breast, grilled and chopped
- ½ avocado, peeled, de-seeded and chopped
- 1 small carrot, finely grated
- Squeeze of fresh lime juice
- 1 tsp pine nuts

Method

1 Spread the dairy-free mayonnaise on the wraps.

2 Sprinkle the watercress on one half of the wrap.

3 Add in the chicken, avocado and carrot.

4 Squeeze across a splash of fresh lime juice and top with pine nuts.

5 Roll the wrap up and serve.

CHEF'S NOTE

Sprouted wheat wraps are now widely available in health food stores and provide a great, healthier alternative to traditional refined flours.

HOMEMADE PEANUT BUTTER ON CRISP BREAD

Ingredients

- 2 tbsp Tahini butter
- 1 tbsp raw agave
- Pinch of sea salt

- 4 slices of crisp bread
- 1 tbsp peanuts, crushed or ground
- 1 tsp pine nuts

Method

1 Simply spoon the Tahini butter into a bowl and gently mix in the raw agave.

2 Continue to stir until the two ingredients are smoothly blended together.

3 Add in a very small pinch of sea salt to season and stir again well.

4 Spread the peanut butter on the crisp bread and sprinkle across the crushed or ground peanuts.

5 Top with a sprinkling of pine nuts to serve.

CHEF'S NOTE

This homemade, alkaline version of peanut butter makes a tasty lunchtime treat.

RAINBOW WRAP

Ingredients

- 2 sprouted wheat wraps
- 2 tbsp homemade hummus (p90)
- 1 handful of watercress
- ½ cucumber, sliced into strips
- ¼ yellow pepper, finely sliced into strips
- ½ carrot, finely chopped into strips or grated
- ¼ red pepper, de-seeded & finely chopped into strips
- ½ cooked beetroot, chopped

Method

1 Spread the hummus across the wrap.

2 Arrange the chopped vegetables and salad so they are aligned in colour order according to the colours of the rainbow; green, yellow, orange, red and purple.

3 Roll the wrap up to your preferred style and serve.

CHEF'S NOTE
Serve with a side of homemade roasted vegetable crisps.

SMOKED SALMON AND CUCUMBER OPEN SANDWICH

Ingredients

- 2 Seeded, gluten free flatbreads
- 1 tbsp soya spread
- Handful of cucumber slices
- 50g/2oz fresh, smoked salmon
- Freshly chopped dill to garnish
- A squeeze of fresh lemon juice
- Freshly ground black pepper

Method

1 Lightly spread the flatbreads with the soya spread.

2 Place the sliced cucumber on top so the flatbread is evenly covered.

3 Add the smoked salmon on top and garnish with freshly chopped dill.

4 Gently squeeze a drizzle of fresh lemon juice across to flavour and add plenty of black pepper.

CHEF'S NOTE

Always try to purchase the fish as fresh as possible and eat the same day.

PRAWN AND AVOCADO CRISPBREAD

Ingredients

- 100g/3½ oz fresh prawns, drained, cooked, peeled and de-tailed
- 1 small avocado, peeled, de-stoned & chopped
- 1 tbsp homemade mayonnaise (p93)
- 1 tsp freshly squeezed lemon juice
- Sea salt and pepper to season
- 4 Slices of crisp bread
- Freshly chopped Dill to garnish

Method

1 Place the prawns in a bowl with the avocado and spoon in the homemade mayonnaise.

2 Mix the ingredients until the prawns and avocado are evenly covered.

3 Add in the lemon juice and salt and pepper to season and mix well again.

4 Spoon on to the crisp bread and sprinkle on top fresh dill to garnish.

CHEF'S NOTE

For an on-the-go option, use the prawn and avocado option as a filling for a gluten-free bread sandwich.

SWEET POTATO JACKET AND HUMMUS

Ingredients

- 1 tsp Flaxseed Oil
- 1 Sweet Potato
- Sea Salt to Season

- 1 tbsp homemade hummus (p90)
- 1 tsp Sunflower Seeds
- 1 tsp Pumpkin Seeds

Method

1 Pre-heat the oven to 180C/350F/Gas4..

2 Pierce the potato several times with a knife and then rub the oil all over the potato.

3 Place on a baking tray and season with sea salt.

4 Cook for 45 minutes (or until the inside is sift), rotating the potato half way through.

5 Remove from the oven and slice the potato open.

6 Spoon in the homemade hummus and top with the seeds.

CHEF'S NOTE
Serve with a small portion of homemade coleslaw (p95) and fresh salad.

GRILLED CHICKEN AND PESTO WRAP

Ingredients

- 2 sprouted wheat wraps
- 1 tbsp homemade green pesto (p92)
- 2 handfuls fresh baby leaf salad
- Small handful of alfalfa sprouts
- 1 chicken breast, grilled and chopped
- 1 tsp pine nuts
- 1 tsp flax seeds
- Splash of freshly squeezed lime juice

Method

1 Spread the green pesto across the wraps and place the salad and sprouts to one side.

2 Lay on top the grilled chicken pieces and drizzle any leftover, or extra if preferred, green pesto over them.

3 Sprinkle on top the pine nuts and flax seeds.

4 Add a splash of fresh lime juice and roll to serve.

CHEF'S NOTE

For an occasional treat, add a light sprinkling of fresh Parmesan.

TOMATO AND PEPPER FLATBREAD

Ingredients

- 1 tbsp flaxseed oil
- 1 large, tomato, finely chopped
- ¼ red onion, finely chopped
- ¼ red pepper, finely chopped
- 2 tbsp passata

- ½ tsp paprika
- ½ tsp chilli powder
- 1 tbsp chia seeds
- 2 seeded, gluten-free flatbreads

Method

1 Warm the oil in a saucepan.

2 Add in the tomato, red onion and red pepper and cook on a medium heat for 5 minutes or until they start to soften.

3 Add in the passata, paprika and chilli powder and warm through.

4 Lightly toast or grill the flatbread and spoon the tomato and pepper mixture on top.

5 Sprinkle over the chia seeds to serve.

CHEF'S NOTE

Serve with a side of fresh salad. For an occasional treat, add a slice of cooked lean bacon into the mixture with the fat removed.

Salad
RECIPES

Time to try....

MANGO AND AVOCADO SALAD

·············· *Ingredients* ··············

- 1 tbsp olive oil
- ½ tsp freshly squeezed lime juice
- ½ tsp freshly squeezed lemon juice
- 125g/4oz fresh baby leaf salad
- 1 ripe mango, peeled and chopped

- 1 ripe avocado, peeled, de-stoned & chopped
- 1 tbsp pine nuts
- 1 tbsp chia seeds

·············· *Method* ··············

1 Mix the olive oil with the lime and lemon juice to make a dressing then put to one side.

2 Toss the salad leaves, mango and avocado in a bowl ready to serve.

3 Drizzle over the dressing and sprinkle across the pine nuts and chia seeds to serve.

CHEF'S NOTE
Mango is a great alkaline ingredient and benefits your entire body; most noticeably it can improve the appearance and overall health of your skin.

SUPER SIMPLE BEETROOT SALAD

Ingredients

- 1 iceberg lettuce, chopped
- 1 red onion, finely chopped
- 1 cooked beetroot, finely chopped
- 1 tbsp chia seeds
- 1 tbsp sunflower seeds

Method

1 Toss the lettuce and red onion in a bowl together.

2 Add the beetroot on top of the salad.

3 Sprinkle over the seeds and serve.

CHEF'S NOTE

Add a salad dressing of choice to this if desired, although the beetroot should provide sufficient flavour and moisture, however ensure the dressing is simple and homemade to avoid too much acidity.

SWEET POTATO, BEETROOT AND GOAT'S CHEESE SALAD

Ingredients

- 200g/7oz sweet potatoes, peeled and chopped
- 1 tsp flaxseed oil
- Pinch of sea salt
- ½ tbsp olive oil
- ½ tsp freshly squeezed lemon juice

- Small pinch of sea salt and pepper
- 100g/3½oz fresh Rocket Leaves
- 1 medium cooked beetroot, cubed
- 50g/2oz fresh goat's cheese, crumbled
- 1 tbsp pumpkin seeds

Method

1 Pre-heat the oven to 180C/350F/Gas4.

2 Place the chopped sweet potatoes on a baking tray and drizzle the oil over them. Season with sea salt and roast for 30 – 35 minutes or until tender.

3 Mix the olive oil, lemon juice and salt & pepper together to create a light dressing and put to one side.

4 Place the rocket leaves in a bowl and then add in the sweet potatoes, beetroot and goat's cheese.

5 Toss the ingredients together and drizzle on some of the salad dressing.

6 Serve topped with the pumpkin seeds.

CHEF'S NOTE
Adding sweet potatoes to a salad keeps you feeling fuller for longer and adds a little sweetness without compromising the alkalinity of the meal.

TUNA AND THREE BEAN SALAD

Ingredients

- 1 tsp linseed oil
- 1 small, fresh tuna steak
- Sea salt and pepper
- 100g/3½ oz fresh baby leaf salad
- 50g/2oz soy beans, cooked or tinned
- 50g/2oz red kidney beans, cooked or tinned
- 50g/2oz lima beans, cooked or tinned
- ½ red onion, peeled and chopped
- 1 tsp red wine vinegar

Method

1 Heat the oil in a pan and cook the tuna steak on a medium heat.

2 Cook to your preference (90 seconds each side for rare) and place to one side.

3 Toss the baby leaf salad, beans and red onions in a bowl ready to serve.

4 Break the tuna steak up and place on top of the salad.

5 Drizzle the red wine vinegar on top to serve.

CHEF'S NOTE

Make sure the tuna is bought fresh and ideally cooked the same day as purchase to ensure the maximum nutrients are obtained.

CHICKPEA AND PEPPER SALAD

Ingredients

- 2 tsp olive oil
- ½ tsp freshly squeezed lemon juice
- Small pinch of sea salt and pepper
- 300g/11oz tinned chickpeas, drained
- 2 handfuls spinach leaves
- 1 red pepper, de-seeded and chopped

- 50g/2oz sweetcorn, cooked
- 1 tbsp fresh coriander, chopped
- 1 tsp paprika
- 1 tbsp chia seeds
- 1 tbsp pumpkin seeds

Method

1 Mix the olive oil, lemon juice and salt and pepper together to create a light dressing and place to one side.

2 Toss the chickpeas, red pepper and sweetcorn in a bowl together.

3 Stir in the coriander, paprika and seeds.

4 Pile on top of the spinach leaves and drizzle over the pre-prepared salad dressing.

5 Garnish with a small sprig of coriander.

CHEF'S NOTE
Chickpeas make a fantastic base for a filling salad, while red peppers are an excellent source of Vitamin C.

CHICKEN, AVOCADO AND ALFALFA SALAD

Ingredients

- 1 tbsp olive oil
- ½ tsp freshly squeezed lime juice
- 75g/3oz fresh watercress
- 50g/2oz fresh alfalfa sprouts
- 1 cucumber, cubed

- 1 ripe avocado, peeled, de-stoned and chopped
- 1 chicken breast, grilled and chopped
- 1 tbsp cashew nuts
- 1 tbsp pine nuts

Method

1 Mix the olive oil and lime juice together to create a light dressing and place to one side.

2 Toss the watercress, sprouts, avocado and cucumber in a bowl together ready to serve.

3 Place the chicken on top of the tossed salad and drizzle the prepared dressing over the top.

4 Sprinkle over the nuts and serve.

CHEF'S NOTE
Use a coffee grinder or pestle and mortar to grind the nuts before adding to a salad if you wish.

TOMATO AND OLIVE SALAD

Ingredients

- 1 tbsp olive oil
- 1 tbsp red wine vinegar
- ¼ tsp freshly squeezed lime juice
- ½ garlic clove, crushed
- 1 tsp mild chilli powder
- 3 large tomatoes, chopped

- 75g/3oz fresh, pitted olives
- ½ cucumber, cubed
- 1 large chicory head
- 1 tsp pine nuts
- 1 tsp sesame seeds

Method

1 Add the oil, red wine vinegar, lime juice, garlic, chilli powder, tomatoes, olives and cucumber into a bowl and mix well together.

2 Separate the leaves of the chicory head to prepare a base for the dressed salad.

3 Spoon the tomato and olive salad mixture on top of the chicory.

4 Sprinkle over the nuts and seeds to serve.

CHEF'S NOTE
Replace the olives with nectarines for a sweeter, summery alternative.

ARTICHOKE AND WALNUT SALAD

Ingredients

- 200g/7oz artichoke hearts
- 150g/5oz asparagus, chopped
- 1 tbsp walnut oil
- 1 tsp freshly squeezed orange juice

- 100g/3½ oz fresh mixed salad
- A handful of alfalfa sprouts
- 50g/2oz walnuts

Method

1 Cook the Artichoke in boiling water on a medium heat for approx. 20 mins or until tender.

2 Add in the asparagus and cook for just a couple of minutes until tender.

3 While the vegetables cook, mix the walnut oil with the orange juice to create a light salad dressing and place to one side to serve.

4 Remove the artichokes and asparagus from the heat and drain.

5 Mix the salad with the alfalfa sprouts, and then add in the artichokes and asparagus. Drizzle over the prepared oil dressing and top with walnuts to serve.

CHEF'S NOTE
To reduce cooking time, used tinned artichoke hearts for an on-the-go alternative.

ORANGE AND FENNEL SALAD

Ingredients

- 1 tbsp olive oil
- ½ tsp freshly squeezed orange juice
- 2 large, ripe oranges, peeled
- 1 small fennel bulb, finely chopped
- ½ onion, peeled and roughly chopped
- ½ tsp fresh parsley, finely chopped
- 1 tbsp sunflower seeds
- 1 tsp linseeds

Method

1 Mix the olive oil and orange juice together to make a light dressing and place to one side ready to serve.

2 Add the orange segments, onion and fennel to a bowl.

3 Drizzle over the salad dressing and toss the ingredients so they are evenly covered.

4 Add in the fresh parsley and seeds and mix again before serving.

CHEF'S NOTE

To get your taste buds tingling, add in some fresh red chilli to give the salad a powerful kick.

WARM GREEN BEAN SALAD

Ingredients

- 75g/3oz fresh green beans, chopped
- 50g/2oz fresh mangetout
- 50g/2oz tinned broad beans
- ½ tbsp olive oil

- ½ tsp freshly squeezed Lemon Juice
- ½ garlic clove, crushed
- 25g/1oz peanuts, ground
- 1 tbsp pine nuts

Method

1 Boil the green beans and mangetout for a few minutes or until tender.

2 Add the broad beans to the pan for a minute to warm through.

3 Drain and place to one side.

4 Mix together the olive oil, lemon juice and the garlic.

5 Combine with the green beans, mangetout and broad beans until evenly coated.

6 Add in the ground peanuts and pine nuts before serving.

CHEF'S NOTE

Green beans help to eliminate toxins from the body, boost energy levels and help to optimize the digestive system.

Dinner
RECIPES

Time to try.....

TRADITIONAL BEEF CASSEROLE

Ingredients

- 1 tbsp flaxseed oil
- ½ onion, finely chopped
- 250g/9oz lean beef, diced
- 2 medium carrots, chopped
- 1 large sweet potato, peeled & chopped
- 1 parsnip, chopped
- 1 tbsp pearl barley
- Sea salt and pepper to season
- A dash of red wine

Method

1 Pre-heat the oven to 180C/350F/Gas4.

2 Heat the oil in a saucepan. Add the onions and gently cook for a few minutes until softened.

3 Remove the onions, increase the heat, add in the beef and cook until sealed.

4 Remove from the heat and place the beef in a casserole dish along with everything else.

5 Cook for one hour or until everything is tender and piping hot.

CHEF'S NOTE
This recipe is slow cooker suitable to make busy lifestyles easier; serve with organic green beans and cabbage.

FENNEL AND DILL PORK

·············· *Ingredients* ··············

- 2 lean pork chops, fat removed
- ½ fresh fennel bulb, finely chopped
- ½ apple, cored & chopped
- 1 carrot, chopped

- 1 tsp freshly chopped dill
- Pinch of pepper
- 150ml/5floz vegetable stock
- Handful of new potatoes, halved

·············· *Method* ··············

1 Pre-heat the oven to 150C/300F/Gas2.

2 Sear the pork chops in a pan on a medium heat before placing in a roasting tin or dish.

3 Add the remaining ingredients to the dish, cover, and cook for 1½ hours. Or until tender.

4 Remove from the oven and place the pork chops on a plate to serve, topped with the cooked apples.

5 Spoon out the apples and use the remaining stock mixture to drizzle on top of the pork as a gravy alternative to serve.

CHEF'S NOTE
Serve with your choice of fresh, seasonal green vegetables.

VEGETARIAN BEAN CHILLI

Ingredients

- 1 tsp almond butter
- ½ red onion, chopped
- ½ red pepper, chopped
- 1 garlic clove, crushed
- 1 tbsp tomato puree
- 1 tsp chilli powder
- 1 tsp paprika
- ¼ fresh red chilli, de-seeded & finely chopped
- 150ml/5floz vegetable stock
- 200g/7oz fresh tomatoes, chopped
- 100g/3½oz kidney beans
- 100g/3½oz lima (white) beans
- Sea salt & pepper to season
- Parsley to garnish

Method

1 Melt the almond butter in a saucepan and add in the red onion, red pepper and garlic.

2 Cook for 5 minutes on a medium heat.

3 Add in the tomato puree, chilli powder, paprika and chilli and stir well until the vegetables are evenly covered.

4 Add in the vegetable stock, beans and salt and pepper to season, stirring well.

5 Reduce to a low heat and cook for 15 to 20 minutes.

6 Garnish with parsley to serve.

CHEF'S NOTE
Serve with organic brown rice or freshly cooked quinoa.

SWEET POTATO CURRY

Ingredients

- 1 tsp flaxseed oil
- 1 red onion, peeled and chopped
- 2 large sweet potatoes, peeled & cubed
- 2 garlic cloves, minced
- 350g/12oz tomatoes, chopped
- 400ml/14oz coconut milk
- Bunch of fresh coriander, finely chopped

- ½ tsp fresh root ginger, grated
- 1 small red chilli, de-seeded & finely chopped
- 1 tbsp red lentils
- 1 tbsp curry powder
- Sea salt & pepper to season

Method

1 Warm the oil in a saucepan over a medium heat.

2 Add in the onion and stir for 1–2 minutes.

3 Add in the sweet potato and garlic and stir for a further 5 minutes.

4 Add in the tomatoes and coconut milk and bring to simmer.

5 Add in the remaining ingredients, stirring well, and allow to simmer on a medium to low heat for 20 – 25 minutes, or until the potatoes are tender.

6 Garnish with a few leftover coriander leaves to garnish.

CHEF'S NOTE

Spoon a little coconut cream on top to serve for a creamier finish.

TOMATO PESTO PASTA

Ingredients

- 150g/5oz gluten-free pasta
- Pinch of sea salt
- 2 tbsp homemade red tomato pesto (p94)
- 3 large fresh tomatoes, chopped
- 2 slices lean bacon with the fat removed, grilled and chopped
- Fresh basil leaves to garnish

Method

1 Bring a pan of water to boil and add in the pasta with a pinch of salt.

2 Cook for 10-12 minutes or until the pasta is cooked through.

3 Remove the pan from the heat, drain and return the pasta to the pan.

4 Mix in the homemade pesto and bacon and return to the heat.

5 Stir well until warmed through.

6 Add the crunchy fresh tomatoes, garnish with fresh basil leaves to serve.

CHEF'S NOTE
Use any leftovers for lunch the following day.

HUMMUS CHICKEN WITH SWEET POTATO WEDGES

Ingredients

- 2 chicken breasts
- 1 tbsp homemade hummus (p90)
- Sea salt and pepper
- 1 tsp freshly chopped rosemary
- 1 tsp flaxseeds
- 2 large sweet potatoes, peeled & chopped
- 2 tsp flaxseed oil

Method

1 Pre-heat the oven to 180C./350F/Gas4.

2 Cut a square of tin foil for each fillet, large enough to wrap and cover it.

3 Spread the hummus on top of the chicken fillets and sprinkle over the sea salt and pepper to season as well as the rosemary and flaxseeds.

4 Seal the tin foil and place the wrapped fillets on a baking tray.

5 Coat the sweet potato wedges in the oil, season with a little sea salt and place both trays in the oven. Cook for 30 minutes.

6 Remove from the chicken fillets from the oven and open the tin foil to allow the hummus to roast slightly.

7 Place back in the oven and cook for a further 10-15 minutes or until the chicken is cooked through and the wedges are tender.

CHEF'S NOTE
Serve with fresh organic seasonal greens or quinoa if preferred.

STEAMED LEMON SALMON

Ingredients

- 2 fresh salmon fillets
- ½ fresh lemon
- 1 tsp flaxseeds
- 1 tsp linseeds
- 1 tsp dried mixed herbs
- Large pinch sea salt and pepper

Method

1 Pre-heat the oven to 180C/350F/Gas4.

2 Place the salmon fillets on sheets of tin foil, separately, large enough to wrap and cover the salmon.

3 Give a good squeeze of the lemon, collecting the juice in a bowl.

4 Add into the bowl the seeds, herbs and salt and pepper and gently mix.

5 Drizzle over the salmon fillets and then seal the tin foil so the salmon is completely covered.

6 Place on a baking tray and put in the oven to steam for 20 minutes, or until the salmon is cooked through.

7 Remove from the oven and take the salmon out of the tin foil to serve.

8 Collect the remaining juices from the tin foil and use to drizzle over the salmon to serve.

CHEF'S NOTE
Serve with homemade agave roasted vegetables (p96) or your choice of steamed seasonal greens.

SEVEN SEEDED GREENS

Ingredients

- 2 handfuls broccoli florets
- 50g/2oz green beans, chopped
- 50g/2oz broad beans
- 50g/2oz asparagus spears, chopped
- Large handful of kale
- 50g/2oz frozen peas
- 1 tbsp almond butter

- 1 tsp sunflower seeds, pre-soaked
- 1 tsp pumpkin seeds, pre-soaked
- 1 tsp alfalfa sprouts, pre-soaked
- ½ tsp sesame seeds, pre-soaked
- ½ tsp poppy seeds, pre-soaked
- ½ tsp linseed, pre-soaked
- ½ tsp millet seeds, pre-soaked

Method

1 Bring a large saucepan of water to boil.

2 Add in the broccoli, green beans, broad beans and asparagus and boil for 10–12 minutes.

3 Add in the kale and peas and boil for a further 10-12 minutes or until the vegetables are tender.

4 Drain the vegetables and then place them back in the saucepan.

5 Add in the almond butter and stir into the vegetables until it has completely melted; place the pan back over a low heat if required.

6 Sprinkle in the pre-soaked seeds and mix well before serving.

CHEF'S NOTE
Soaking nuts and seeds make them easier to digest. Just leave in salted filtered water for approx 7 hours.

QUINOA STUFFED PEPPERS

Ingredients

- 600ml/1pt vegetable stock
- 50g/2oz quinoa
- 1 tsp hempseed oil
- 1 tomato, finely chopped
- ½ red onion, finely chopped
- ½ courgette, finely chopped
- 1 garlic clove, crushed
- 1 tsp pine nuts
- 2 peppers, the top removed and de-seeded

Method

1 Pre-heat the oven to 180C./350F/Gas4.

2 Bring the vegetable stock to boil.

3 Add the quinoa and boil for 20 minutes.

4 Pour the hempseed oil into a saucepan on a medium heat and add in the tomato, onion, courgette and garlic.

5 Sauté for 5 minutes or until the vegetables have softened.

6 Remove from the heat and place to one side.

7 Once cooked, drain and rinse the quinoa. Add the sautéed vegetables and pine nuts to the quinoa and stir well.

8 Spoon the mixture into the bell peppers.

9 Place the peppers on a baking tray and cook in the oven for 15-20 minutes or until the peppers are tender.

CHEF'S NOTE

Serve with a large fresh green salad and homemade mayonnaise (p93).

FILLET STEAK WITH GARLIC BUTTER

Ingredients

- 1 tsp almond butter
- ½ tsp fresh garlic, minced
- 1 tsp soya butter

- 2 lean, fillet steaks
- Sea salt and pepper to season
- Fresh parsley to garnish

Method

1 In a small bowl, thoroughly mix the minced garlic into 1 tsp of almond butter and place to one side, ready to serve.

2 Then melt 1 tsp of soya butter in a pan on a medium heat. Place the fillet steaks on a chopping board and gently bash with a rolling pin to flatten them out slightly.

3 Rub both sides of the steaks with salt and pepper to season. Add the steaks to the pan and cook to your preferred rarity, turning and sealing the steaks as appropriate.

4 Remove from the heat and serve. Spoon the garlic butter on top and allow it to melt. Garnish with a fresh parsley leaves.

CHEF'S NOTE
Serve with sweet potato wedges and leftover, or fresh, seven seeded greens (p53).

WARM ROASTED BEETROOT SALAD

Ingredients

- 2 large beetroot, quartered
- 1 courgette, sliced
- ½ small butternut squash, peeled and chopped
- 1 red onion, peeled and roughly chopped
- 1 tsp hempseed oil
- Sea salt to season

- 2 large handfuls of fresh rocket leaves
- 1 carrot, grated
- 50g/2oz goat's cheese
- 1 tsp chia seeds
- 1 tbsp pumpkin seeds
- 1 tsp pine nuts

Method

1 Pre-heat the oven to 180C/350F/Gas4.

2 Place the beetroot, courgette, butternut squash and red onion in a roasting dish and drizzle over the hempseed oil, turning the vegetables so they are evenly covered. Add a pinch of sea salt to season.

3 Place in the oven and roast for 35-40 minutes, or until the vegetables have cooked through.

4 Once cooked, place the vegetables on top of a bed of rocket leaves. Add on top the grated carrot and goat's cheese and toss the salad well.

5 Sprinkle over the seeds and nuts and lightly toss once more before serving.

CHEF'S NOTE
Drizzle over a light homemade dressing or simply use some of the juices from the roasting dish.

ROASTED BUTTERNUT SQUASH 'RISOTTO'

Ingredients

- 1 carrot, cubed
- ½ butternut squash, peeled and cubed
- 1 tsp olive oil
- Sea salt to season
- 1 Lt/1½pt vegetable stock
- 150g/5oz quinoa

- ½ tsp freshly squeezed lemon juice
- 1 tbsp curry powder
- 2 tsp mild chilli powder
- ½ tsp nutmeg
- 75ml/3floz soy cream
- Fresh coriander to garnish

Method

1 Pre-heat the oven to 180C/350F/Gas4.

2 Drizzle the oil over the chopped vegetables and season with sea salt. Place in the oven for 30-35 minutes or until the vegetables are tender.

3 Meanwhile, bring the water to boil in a saucepan. Add in the quinoa and simmer for 10 minutes, stirring continuously. Allow to simmer for a further 5 minutes, or until the quinoa is fully cooked and expanded.

4 When cooked, remove the quinoa from the heat and add in the lemon juice, curry and chilli powder and nutmeg and stir well.

5 Mix in the cooked roasted vegetables, followed by the soy cream and return to a very low heat for 1 – 2 minutes, stirring continuously.

6 Remove from the heat and serve garnished with freshly chopped coriander.

CHEF'S NOTE

For a 'one pot' option, boil the vegetables in the water before adding in the quinoa.

LEMON AND GARLIC COD

·········· *Ingredients* ··········

- 2 garlic cloves, crushed
- 1 tsp freshly squeezed lemon juice
- 2 tsp olive oil
- Pinch of dried chilli flakes

- 2 fresh cod fillets
- 1 lemon, quartered
- ½ tbsp parsley, freshly chopped
- Sea salt and pepper to season

·········· *Method* ··········

1 Pre-heat the oven to 180C/350F/Gas4.

2 Mix in a bowl the garlic, lemon juice, oil and chilli flakes.

3 Coat the cod fillets in the lemon and garlic oil mixture and place the fillets on a sheet of tin foil big enough to wrap and cover them.

4 Add in the lemon quarters, sprinkle on top the freshly chopped parsley and season with pinch of sea salt and pepper.

5 Fold the foil over so the fillets are completely covered and can steam to cook.

6 Cook in the oven for 15 – 20 minutes or until the cod is cooked through.

7 Garnish with any leftover fresh parsley leaf.

CHEF'S NOTE

For extra flavour, allow the cod to marinate for 2 – 3 hours in the fridge in the garlic and lemon oils. Serve with crushed baby potatoes or a side of quinoa.

Soup
RECIPES

Time to try.....

CARROT AND CORIANDER SOUP

Ingredients

- 600ml/1pt vegetable stock
- 4 large carrots, chopped
- ½ onion, diced
- 1 medium potato, chopped
- 3 tbsp fresh coriander, chopped
- 1 tsp paprika, dried
- A pinch of sea salt

Method

1 Bring the vegetable stock to boil.

2 Add the carrots, onion and potato to the stock and boil for 10 minutes.

3 Stir in the coriander, paprika and salt & simmer until tender.

4 Use a hand blender or food processor to blend until you have a smooth, lump-free texture.

5 Serve with a little additional coriander garnish.

CHEF'S NOTE

Carrot is a nutritious root vegetable and provides a wealth of vitamins, minerals and antioxidants; it is highly alkaline and a great soup base for a warming lunch or light dinner.

POTATO AND LEEK SOUP

Ingredients

- 600ml/1pt vegetable stock
- 2 leeks, chopped
- 3 medium potatoes, peeled & diced
- ½ onion, diced

- 150ml/5floz goat's milk
- 1 tsp mixed fresh herbs, finely chopped
- Large pinch sea salt and pepper

Method

1 Bring the vegetable stock to boil.

2 Add the leeks, potatoes and onion to the stock and boil for 20 minutes or until everything is tender.

3 Pour in the goat's milk, season with the mixed herbs and gently warm through.

4 Use a hand blender or food processor to blend until you have a smooth, lump-free texture.

5 Check the seasoning and serve.

CHEF'S NOTE

Goat's milk is a great alternative to traditional cream or milk in soups; it is much easier for our bodies to digest than cow's milk and is often used as an effective anti-inflammatory.

CHUNKY WINTER VEGETABLE SOUP

Ingredients

- 600ml/1pt vegetable stock
- ½ onion, diced
- 1 large carrot, diced
- 1 celery stick, chopped
- 1 small potato, peeled and diced
- 1 tbsp pearl barley
- 1 tsp dried red lentils
- Sea salt and pepper to season
- Freshly chopped parsley to serve

Method

1 Bring the vegetable stock to boil.

2 Add the mixed vegetables to the stock and boil for 10 minutes. Add in the pearl barley and lentils and continue to boil until the vegetables are tender and the lentils have softened. Season with salt and pepper.

3 Use a hand blender or food processor to roughly blend leaving a chunky mixture. Serve with a Parsley garnish.

CHEF'S NOTE

Pearl barley can help digestion problems and also aid weight loss and management. Like many other lentils, it can thicken soups and casseroles and provide good quality fibre keeping you feel fuller for longer.

CHILLI AND CAULIFLOWER SOUP

Ingredients

- 600ml/1pt vegetable stock
- ½ small onion, diced
- ½ cauliflower head, chopped
- 1 potato, peeled and chopped
- ¼ small, fresh red chilli, de-seeded & finely chopped
- ½ clove of garlic, minced

- ½ tsp paprika
- 1 tsp cumin
- ½ tsp allspice
- Large pinch sea salt and pepper
- Sprinkling of vegan parmesan to serve, finely grated

Method

1 Bring the stock to boil.

2 Add the onion, cauliflower and potato to the stock and simmer for 5 minutes.

3 Add in the chilli and garlic, stir well and cook for a further 5 minutes. Sprinkle in the paprika, cumin and allspice and season with sea salt and pepper.

4 Simmer for a further 10 to 15 minutes or until the vegetables are tender.

5 Use a hand blender or food processor to blend until you have a smooth, lump-free texture.

6 Serve with a sprinkling of vegan parmesan on top.

CHEF'S NOTE

Cauliflower is a great alkaline food and helps your body to absorb iron more efficiently.

BROCCOLI AND GOAT'S CHEESE SOUP

Ingredients

- 600ml/1pt vegetable stock
- ½ onion, diced
- 1 garlic clove, crushed
- 1 medium head of broccoli
- 1 potato, peeled & chopped
- 1 tsp fresh mixed herbs
- Sea salt and pepper to season
- 75g/3oz fresh goat's cheese
- Freshly chopped parsley to garnish

Method

1 Bring the stock to boil.

2 Add the onion, garlic and broccoli into the saucepan and bring to boil.

3 Add in the mixed herbs and salt and pepper and simmer for 15 – 20 minutes or until the broccoli is tender.

4 Keep the saucepan on a low heat and add in a small amount of the goat's cheese. Use a hand blender or food processor to blend until you have a smooth, lump-free texture.

5 Add in some more of the goat's cheese and blend again. Repeat until all the goat's cheese has been added in. Serve with a parsley garnish and any left over crumbled goat's cheese.

CHEF'S NOTE
Rich in vitamins, Goat's Cheese is also an excellent source of phosphorous and adds depth of flavour to any recipe.

SPICED PUMPKIN SOUP

Ingredients

- 600ml/1pt vegetable stock
- 1 small potato, peeled and cubed
- 1 carrot, peeled and cubed
- 800g/1¾lb pumpkin, peeled, de-seeded and cubed
- ½ tsp nutmeg

- 1 tsp cumin
- ¼ tsp allspice
- 150ml/5floz nut milk
- Sea salt and pepper to season
- 1 tbsp pumpkin seeds, chopped

Method

1 Bring the stock to the boil.

2 Add the potato, carrot and pumpkin to the stock and simmer for 10 minutes.

3 Add in the spices and allow the soup to simmer for a further 10 – 15 minutes or until the vegetables are tender.

4 Keeping on a low heat, stir in the nut milk and season with sea salt and pepper. Use a hand blender or food processor to blend until you have a smooth, lump-free texture. Sprinkle the pumpkin seeds on top to serve.

CHEF'S NOTE

Drizzle some soya cream on top of the soup to serve as a healthier alternative to traditional, fatty cream if desired.

PARSNIP AND GINGER SOUP

Ingredients

- 600ml/1pt vegetable stock
- 1 small onion, diced
- 4 parsnips, peeled and chopped
- ½ garlic clove, crushed
- 1 tsp fresh root ginger, finely grated
- ½ tsp paprika
- Large pinch sea salt and pepper
- 1 tbsp coconut cream
- Chopped parsley to garnish

Method

1 Bring the vegetable stock to boil.

2 Add the onion, parsnips, garlic and ginger and simmer for 10 minutes.

3 Sprinkle in the paprika and salt and pepper to season and stir well.

4 Allow to cook for a further 15 – 20 minutes or until the parsnips are tender.

5 Use a hand blender or food processor to blend until you have a smooth, lump-free texture.

6 Either stir in the coconut cream or drizzle on top to finish. Serve with a parsley garnish.

CHEF'S NOTE

Parsnips have been linked to a number of health benefits, from heart health to brain functionality, as well as helping to improve and enhance eyesight health.

KALE AND LENTIL SOUP

Ingredients

- 600ml/1pt vegetable stock
- 1 medium potato, peeled & chopped
- ½ onion, diced
- 1 celery stick, chopped
- 125g/4oz kale

- 1 tbsp lentils
- 1 tbsp yellow split peas
- Sea salt and pepper to season
- Pinch of chilli flakes

Method

1 Bring the vegetable stock to boil.

2 Add the potato, onion and celery and simmer for 10 minutes.

3 Add in the kale, lentils and split peas & cook for a further 15 minutes, or until the kale has softened to tender.

4 Season with salt and pepper, then use a hand blender or food processor to blend until you have a smooth, lump-free texture.

5 Pour into a bowl and sprinkle the chilli flakes on top to serve.

CHEF'S NOTE

Kale is a good source of fibre, helping you feel fuller for longer and is packed with vitamins and minerals key for aiding digestion, health and wellbeing.

BEETROOT AND GINGER SOUP

Ingredients

- 600ml/1 pint vegetable stock
- 1 potato, peeled and chopped
- ½ small onion, peeled and chopped
- 125g/4oz fresh tomatoes, chopped
- 150g/5oz beetroot, grated

- ¾ tbsp fresh root ginger, finely grated
- ½ tsp allspice
- Sea salt and pepper to season
- 1 tsp chia seeds

Method

1 Bring the stock to the boil.

2 Add all the ingredients into the saucepan and boil for 25-30 minutes, or until the vegetables are tender.

3 Season with salt and pepper, then use a hand blender or food processor to blend until you have a smooth, lump-free texture.

4 Sprinkle the chia seeds on top to serve.

CHEF'S NOTE

Beetroot is a powerful antioxidant and is particularly good for hair, nails and skin, as well as improving kidney function and aiding digestion.

Dessert
RECIPES

Time to try....

COCONUT AND FRUIT YOGHURT

Ingredients

- 150ml/5 floz fresh coconut yoghurt
- 1 tbsp coconut flakes
- 100g/3½oz blueberries
- 50g/2oz blackberries
- 1 tbsp chia seeds

Method

1 Simply spoon the fresh coconut yoghurt into a bowl or glass to serve.

2 Either sprinkle the coconut flakes and fruit on top or mix into the yoghurt.

3 Add the chia seeds on top of the mixture and serve.

CHEF'S NOTE
Coconut can be used to treat numerous illnesses and digestive problems; it is an invaluable addition to any diet.

BAKED BANANA

Ingredients

- 1 large, ripe banana
- 1 tsp coconut cream
- 1 tsp coconut flakes

Method

1 Pre-heat the oven to 180C/350F/Gas4.

2 Wrap the banana, still in the skin, in tin foil and place on a baking tray.

3 Cook for 10-15 minutes or until the banana has softened. Remove from tin foil and remove the peel.

4 Place on a plate or bowl ready to serve and accompany with a small dollop of coconut cream.

5 Sprinkle on top coconut flakes to serve.

CHEF'S NOTE
A really quick and simple dessert that will satisfy a sweet tooth.

GRAPEFRUIT AND STRAWBERRY SALAD

Ingredients

- 1 ripe grapefruit, halved
- 100g/3½ oz fresh strawberries, chopped
- 2 kiwis, peeled and chopped
- 2 tsp chia seeds

Method

1 Simply place all of the fruit in a bowl to serve and top with a sprinkling of chia seeds.

2 If preferred, peel the grapefruit and serve segments rather than half the fruit, and then lightly toss in a bowl with the strawberries and kiwi before serving.

CHEF'S NOTE
Add a drizzle of agave syrup or crème fraiche to sweeten the finish.

FESTIVE APPLE CRUMBLE

Ingredients

- 3 apples, peeled, cored & cubed
- 3 tsp unrefined raw sugar
- 1 tbsp currants
- 1 tsp cinnamon
- ½ tsp nutmeg
- 25g/1oz gluten free rolled oats

Method

1 Pre-heat the oven to 180C/350F/Gas4.

2 In a bowl, add in the apple, 2tsp raw sugar, currants, cinnamon and nutmeg and toss the ingredients together until the apple and currants are well covered.

3 Spoon the mixture into a baking dish and top with the rolled oats.

4 Sprinkle the remaining sugar on top of the oats.

5 Bake for 20 minutes or until the fruit is tender and the topping is golden.

CHEF'S NOTE

Serve with a dollop of crème fraiche or vegan ice cream.

CHIA SEED PUDDING

Ingredients

- 250ml/8½floz coconut milk
- 4 tbsp chia seeds
- ½ tbsp honey
- A dash of vanilla extract
- A pinch of coconut flakes

Method

1 Simply place all of the ingredients in a food processor, or use a hand blender, and blend until a smooth mixture is created.

2 Pour the mixture into a glass, bowl or dish to serve. Place in the fridge for at least 4 hours to allow the mixture to set.

3 For best results, allow the mixture to set in the fridge overnight.

CHEF'S NOTE
Serve with fresh organic blueberries and a sprinkling of whole chia seeds.

RED FRUIT PUREE

Ingredients

- 1 tsp almond butter
- 75g/3oz strawberries, finely chopped
- 75g/3oz raspberries, finely chopped
- 75g/3oz currants, chopped

- 2 tbsp filtered water
- 1 tsp agave syrup
- 1 tsp chia seeds
- 1 tsp flaxseeds

Method

1 Gently melt the almond butter in a saucepan on a medium heat.

2 Add in the fruit and water and allow to stew for 7-10 minutes, stirring frequently to aid the fruit to break down

3 Add in the agave syrup and seeds and allow to simmer for another 5-7 minutes or until the fruit has completely softened.

4 Allow to cool a little for a few minutes before serving.

CHEF'S NOTE
Add fresh natural yoghurt as a cooling contrast.

MELON AND BERRIES

Ingredients

- 100g/3½oz watermelon flesh
- 75g/3oz honeydew melon flesh
- 50g/2oz mango, peeled and cubed
- 1 tbsp freshly chopped strawberries
- 1 tbsp freshly chopped blueberries

- 2 tbsp coconut cream
- 1 tsp honey
- 1 tsp coconut flakes
- Fresh mint leaf to garnish

Method

1 Toss all of the fruit in a bowl, mixing well.

2 Add in the coconut cream, honey and coconut flakes, and stir gently, but well, until all the fruit is evenly covered.

3 Garnish with a fresh mint leave to serve.

CHEF'S NOTE
Use any leftovers for breakfast the following morning accompanied by half a grapefruit.

COOL GREEN TEA

Ingredients

- 1 teabag of green tea
- 175ml/6floz filtered water, boiling
- 2 ripe kiwi, peeled and finely chopped
- 1 tsp poppy seeds
- 1 tbsp fresh lychees, peeled, de-seeded & chopped
- A large handful of crushed ice

Method

1 Allow the green tea bag to soak in the boiling water for 5 minutes to make green tea.

2 Squeeze and drain the teabag into the water and place to one side to later discard.

3 Pour the green tea into a blender and add in the fruit and poppy seeds. Blend until a smooth mixture is formed.

4 Place the ice in a glass or bowl and pour the mixture over the ice ready to serve.

CHEF'S NOTE

Freeze any leftover mixture in ice cube racks and add to fruit salads.

WATERMELON SORBET

······· *Ingredients* ·······

- ½ watermelon, de-skinned and chopped
- 1 tbsp chia seeds
- 1 tbsp natural yoghurt
- 1 tsp freshly squeezed lemon juice
- ½ tsp freshly chopped mint
- Fresh mint leaf to garnish

······· *Method* ·······

1 Simply place all the ingredients in a food processor or use a hand blender to blend into a smooth mixture.

2 Pour the watermelon mixture into an ice cube tray and freeze into cubes.

3 Once frozen, place the cubes in a plastic bag and smash with a rolling pin to crush the ice.

4 Serve with a fresh mint leaf to garnish.

CHEF'S NOTE
Experiment and try this with other fruits; strawberries also work particularly well.

LEMON BALM AND MANGO CRUSH

Ingredients

- 1 lemon balm tea bag
- 150ml/5floz filtered water, boiling
- 1 large, ripe mango, peeled
- 1 tbsp fresh, natural yoghurt

Method

1 Allow the lemon balm tea bag to infuse in the boiling water for 5 minutes to create lemon balm tea.

2 Squeeze and drain the teabag in the water before discarding.

3 Pour the tea into an ice cube tray and allow to cool before freezing.

4 Once frozen, place the cubes in a plastic bag and smash with a rolling pin to crush the ice.

5 Use a melon baller to scoop the melon into small balls and serve on top of the crushed lemon balm ice.

6 Serve with a spoonful of natural organic yoghurt.

CHEF'S NOTE
This can easily be adapted to use different herbal and fruit teas to suit your preferences for a calming dessert or palate cleanser that works as a brilliant sweet, alkaline alternative.

Snack
RECIPES

Time to try....

ROOT VEGETABLE CRISPS

Ingredients

- 1 tbsp olive oil
- 1 sweet potato, finely sliced
- 1 carrot, finely sliced
- 1 parsnip, finely sliced
- 1 beetroot, finely sliced
- Sea salt and pepper to season

Method

1 Pre-heat the oven to 200C/400F/Gas6.

2 Drizzle the olive oil in a bowl and gently mix with the sliced vegetables.

3 Add in the sea salt and pepper to season and make sure everything is combined really well.

4 Place the sliced vegetables on a baking tray, spreading the slices out into a single layer and cook for 15 to 20 minutes, or until the vegetables are nice and crisp.

CHEF'S NOTE

Cook these in batches and keep in an air tight container to store for a few days – they make a great side addition to a lunchtime salad or wrap.

SUPERCHARGED ZESTY OLIVES

Ingredients

- 1 tbsp olive oil
- 1 garlic clove
- 1 tsp orange zest, finely grated
- 1 tsp lemon zest, finely grated
- 25ml/1fl oz apple cider vinegar
- 1 tsp parsley, freshly chopped

- ½ tsp mint, freshly chopped
- 1 tsp flaxseeds
- ½ tsp fennel seeds
- ¼ tsp caraway seeds
- 1 tsp cumin seeds
- 200g/7oz fresh, pitted olives

Method

1 Crush the garlic clove finely into mince.

2 Mix all ingredients, apart from the olives, in a bowl, stirring well.

3 Add in the olives and gently stir, ensuring the olives are evenly covered in the marinade to serve.

CHEF'S NOTE

This is a brilliantly simple recipe filled with hidden nutrients and is a fantastic addition to any dinner party for guests while they arrive.

PAPRIKA ROASTED ALMONDS

Ingredients

- 2 handfuls of almonds
- 1 tsp flaxseed oil
- Pinch of sea salt
- 1 tsp paprika
- 1 tsp mild chilli powder

Method

1 Pre-heat the oven to 180C/350F/Gas4.

2 Toss the almonds in a bowl with the flaxseed oil, sea salt, paprika and chilli powder.

3 Place on a lined baking tray and cook in the oven for 12 – 15 minutes or until crispy and golden brown.

4 Allow to cool for a few minutes before serving.

CHEF'S NOTE

Try crushing the almonds to create a topping with a kick to finish off a fresh salad.

ROASTED SEEDED ASPARAGUS

Ingredients

- 1 tbsp olive oil
- 1 tsp flaxseeds
- 1 tbsp pumpkin seeds
- 1 tsp linseeds

- 1 garlic clove, crushed
- Sea salt and pepper to season
- 8 asparagus stalks
- 2 tbsp fresh chopped coriander to serve

Method

1 Pre-heat the oven to 200C./400f/Gas6.

2 Mix the olive oil, seeds, garlic, sea salt and pepper in a bowl.

3 Roll the asparagus in the seed oil mixture and lay on a lined baking tray.

4 Roast in the oven for 20–25 minutes or until the asparagus is tender.

5 Cool for a few minutes before serving and garnish with the fresh coriander leaves.

CHEF'S NOTE
Asparagus is a wonderful alkaline addition to any meal or can be a filling snack or light lunch accompaniment and helps to flush excess fluid and salt from the body.

SOAKED ALMONDS

························ *Ingredients* ························

- 2 handfuls of almonds
- Filtered or mineral still water
- Pinch of sea salt

························ *Method* ························

1 Place the almonds in a bowl and pour in enough still water, either filtered or mineral, so that the almonds are comfortably covered.

2 Aim to allow an extra 2cm or more above the level of almonds.

3 Allow to soak overnight, or for a minimum of 8 hours before drying off and eating.

CHEF'S NOTE
Soaking almonds enables them to release an enzyme which specifically aids digestion.

LIME AVOCADO RICE CAKES

Ingredients

- 1 small ripe avocado, peeled & de-stoned
- 1 tsp freshly squeezed lime juice
- Pinch of sea salt and pepper
- 2 wholegrain rice cakes

- Large handful of alfalfa sprouts
- 1 tbsp pine nuts
- 1 tsp sesame seeds
- 1 tsp chilli flakes

Method

1 Use the back of a fork to gently mash the avocado flesh.

2 Combine the mashed avocado with the lime juice, sea salt and pepper and spread over the rice cakes.

3 Sprinkle the sprouts on top, along with the nuts, seeds and chilli flakes to serve.

CHEF'S NOTE

Avocado instantly adds a wealth of antioxidants and nutrients to any snack or meal.

SALSA SALAD

Ingredients

- 2 large ripe tomatoes, finely diced
- ¼ small red onion, finely diced
- ½ small ripe avocado, finely diced
- ¼ cucumber, finely diced
- 1 tbsp fresh mint, finely chopped
- 1 tbsp fresh coriander, finely chopped
- 1 tbsp olive oil
- ½ tsp freshly squeezed lime juice

Method

1 Add all the finely diced fruit and vegetables into a bowl along with the chopped fresh herbs.

2 Drizzle in the olive oil and lime juice and toss the mixture well.

3 Place in a bowl ready to serve.

CHEF'S NOTE

This is a brilliant fresh snack that is easy and quick to prepare. Either eat on its own or add to a rice cake or flat bread for a light lunch.

Homemade
EXTRAS

Time to try....

HOMEMADE HUMMUS

Ingredients

- 150g/5oz tinned chickpeas,
- ½ garlic clove, crushed
- 2 tsp Tahini paste
- 25ml/1floz vegetable stock

- 2 tsp flaxseed oil
- 1 tbsp freshly squeezed lemon juice
- Sea salt and pepper to season

Method

1 Blend together the chickpeas, garlic, Tahini, vegetable stock, oil and lemon juice.

2 Add in sea salt and pepper to season and blend once more.

3 Spoon into a small bowl and place to one side ready to serve.

CHEF'S NOTE

Hummus is a versatile lentil based food that can be used as a spread, dip or topping in a wide variety of snacks and meals.

HOMEMADE SMOOTH PEANUT BUTTER

Ingredients

- 2 tbsp organic Tahini butter
- 1 tbsp raw agave
- Small pinch of sea salt

- 1 tbsp ground peanuts

Method

1 Simply spoon the organic Tahini butter into a bowl and gently mix in the raw agave and ground peanuts..

2 Continue to stir until the ingredients are smoothly blended together.

3 Add in a very small pinch of sea salt to season and stir again well.

CHEF'S NOTE

For a crunchy version, add crushed rather than ground peanuts.

HOMEMADE GREEN PESTO

Ingredients

- 3 tbsp hempseed oil
- 1 large bunch of fresh basil, finely chopped
- 1 garlic clove, crushed
- 3 tbsp pine nuts
- ½ tsp freshly squeezed lemon juice
- Sea salt to season

Method

1 Add all of the ingredients either into a food processor or a bowl if using a hand blender.

2 Blend until you have a smooth, lump free mixture.

3 Place in a bowl to one side ready to use as you please.

CHEF'S NOTE
This is a great alkaline version which can be added to wraps and pasta, or simply used as a dip or dressing.

HOMEMADE MAYONNAISE

Ingredients

- 1 egg
- 1 tsp mustard
- 100ml/7floz olive oil
- 100ml/7floz flaxseed oil

- 60ml/2fl oz linseed oil
- 1 tsp freshly squeezed lemon juice
- Sea salt to season

Method

1 Crack the egg and separate the yolk from the white.

2 Discard of the egg white and place the yolk in a bowl.

3 Add in the remaining ingredients and whisk until a thick consistency appears. Alternatively, used a hand blender to achieve the consistency.

CHEF'S NOTE

Ideally, use the same day as prepared. This can be stored in the fridge in an airtight container but use within one week of preparing.

HOMEMADE RED TOMATO PESTO

Ingredients

- 3 tbsp hempseed oil
- 1 small bunch of fresh basil, finely chopped
- 4 sundried tomatoes
- ½ garlic clove, crushed
- 3 tbsp pine nuts
- ½ tsp freshly squeezed lemon juice
- Sea salt to season

Method

1 Add all of the ingredients either into a food processor, or a bowl if using a hand blender.

2 Blend until you have a smooth, lump free mixture.

3 Place in a bowl to one side ready to use as you please.

CHEF'S NOTE

This is a great alkaline version which can be used as a marinade for meat, or fish, or simply used as a dip or dressing.

HOMEMADE COLESLAW

Ingredients

- 150g/5oz white cabbage, finely chopped
- 2 carrots, grated
- ½ red onion, finely chopped
- 2 tbsp homemade mayonnaise (p93)
- A dash of vinegar
- Sea salt and pepper to season

Method

1 Toss the white cabbage, carrots and red onion in a bowl together until mixed well.

2 Add in the homemade mayonnaise and stir until a combined mixture appears.

3 Add a splash of vinegar and season with sea salt and pepper.

4 Mix well again before serving.

CHEF'S NOTE

This is a great alternative to homemade roasted vegetable crisps with a sandwich or flatbread.

AGAVE ROASTED VEGETABLES

Ingredients

- 1 carrot, cut into batons
- 1 parsnip, cut into batons
- 1 courgette, sliced
- 1 red onion, peeled and chopped
- 1 red pepper, de-seeded and chopped
- 1 tsp freshly chopped thyme

- 1 tsp freshly chopped rosemary
- 1 tsp freshly chopped basil
- 1 tsp sea salt
- ½ tsp ground black pepper
- 1 tbsp agave syrup
- 1 tbsp olive oil

Method

1 Pre-heat the oven to 180C/350F/Gas4.

2 Place all the vegetables in a roasting tray.

3 Add in the herbs, salt and pepper, agave syrup and olive oil and mix well so the vegetables are roughly coated.

4 Roast for 40 minutes, stirring and turning the vegetables half way through.

CHEF'S NOTE

Agave roasted vegetables can be used to recreate an alkaline version of a traditional roast dinner; perfect for colder, winter months.

www.ingramcontent.com/pod-product-compliance
Lightning Source LLC
Chambersburg PA
CBHW081258040426
42452CB00014B/2547

9 781912 511808